DEVOTION

To my lovers

To Him

To my fellow artists

To my friends

To dreaming forever

To my Mother

To my own heart

For having written this

FOREWORD

How much of our futile memory is fact;
How much fiction?

Truly, how thin is the line between Love
& Addiction?

What is destined;
What is Divine Intervention

What is ambition;
But an acceptable obsession?

How much of intimacy, intimate;
How much destructive permission?

What of the future;
Is created by our own self-written prediction?

The Two will not answer these questions
But it will ask them.

THE TWO

A ~~Poetry~~
Study of
Amory
& Duality

By Joseph Colyer

THE TWO: A ~~Poetry~~ Study

By Joseph Colyer

EVERY MORNING

I regain consciousness
To the sound of metal
Scraping against cement
Birds are meant to sing,
But no sound comes through;

Their beaks are sewn shut.

ONE

One.
One could never be enough.

Tragedy is my pornography
& You're still fucking around with handcuffs.

THE END OF THE MANIC PHASE

As it was,
At the end of the manic phase,
There is always an endless panic:
A shuffle away from the deranged
All because
Of the little things:
The falling short of dreams
Unattainable.

WATER, FALL

Endless emotion:
A waterfall

Of sublime sorrow,
Euphoric enigma,
Hope for tomorrow,
And dreadful dystopia.

Life minds
Not at all

Not the absence of horror,
But its sweet embrace,
Not the quest for identity,
But a comfortable place:

A mirrored reflection of your own flawed face.

THE TWO: A ~~Poetry~~ Study

By Joseph Colyer

TRAUMA

We hide our traumas
Like secret dioramas
Collecting dust:
Words we can never say.
But they all sit on display
In our Mind's Museums:
Bitter reasons
To never speak.
But what subtle defeats,
To allow it to become
All that we are:

A slideshow of our own owned horrors

THE MOON

Why sleep
When our dreams reflect the night;
When our shadows can not hide
What we wish to not bring into light?

THE TWO: A ~~Poetry~~ Study

By Joseph Colyer

SNOW

Winter
The sky sniffs cocaine
The shivers make me cry
When it rains
The ground splinters
Under the weight
Of a nervous system
Unplugged & diseased

APHRODITE II

She spoke to me
In a positivity
I hadn't heard before
& I awoke to see
A universe ready
To be reborn

THE TWO: A ~~Poetry~~ Study

By Joseph Colyer

BED

Carry me to bed
So that you can project
Onto me
Whoever it is
You're using me to forget

CANDLES

All it takes is some candles,
A careful, precarious rose,
Add a dash of fright,
& Offer him a glimpse into your window
To that new dimension
That lives within your eyes
So that he'll play the damsel:
And you dish out the lies.
Soon, he'll be at your disposal
He'll worship you between his thighs
& He'll see you in the daylight,
Thinking you only to be fine

His cheeks an intoxicated rose,
& Your Light: his only candle.

THE TWO: A ~~Poetry~~ Study

By Joseph Colyer

HEART

He held a fragment of my heart
And I, a fraction of his
The stars grew nearer
Every moment that we kissed

He held a portion of my mind
I thought I'd never miss
We made worlds, far unholy
As halos danced around our fists

CIRCULAR SAW

I watched the circular saw split my psyche in half
You tied your limbs to bricks of cement

Like an angler fish,
The antenna attached to your head
Drew quite an allure
That came with plenty a false pretense.

But when your appeal did fade,
& I saw the evil behind the lysergic acid
Never fade, day after day,
You knew to drive me to a kingdom far away
Where I played your Queen of Hearts
In your deck containing four suits

Three, as you did choose,
& One, the Spades, you called "Abuse."

THE TWO: A ~~Poetry~~ Study

By Joseph Colyer

THE DEVIL

Your grip is weak
Your stomach is too

Between the sheets,
The Devil
Sure as Hell ain't you.

THIS MUST BE WHAT HEAVEN FEELS LIKE

My head almost touches the ceiling here
This must be what haven feels like:

Four walls;
A floor covered in nails

I walk through fire to get to the bathroom.

IF YOU THINK YOU CAN

You see me,
From skyscrapers
With roots grown deep below
You're thinking of getting swept away
In the forceful undertow
But you won't last a second
That's one thing you should know;
You think you can Love me,
I'm begging you;
For the love of God

Don't.

SHINY, ALUMINUM BOX

Shiny, aluminum box
Shiny, aluminum box
Oh, poor souls,
Left
Unlocked.

THE TWO: A ~~Poetry~~ Study

By Joseph Colyer

EVERY DAY

I walk the streets
I was scared to before
Everything is alive
& so much more.

A woman tends her flowers
A man smiles as I saunter
His way
Why can't it be this easy
To leave the house
Every day?

LIQUIFIED; SKYBOUND

You are drenched in sweat
Delectable
The neon city guides us home
& birds liquify
Skybound
Your body is either a desert
Or a tombstone.
Both expansive
Beyond definition
My fingers climb
Across your skin
To taste the nectar lined within
The stars mark the hallway
To the places we've called prison
Careful notes
Marking our ascent
To comfortable forts
Made of cement
Bunkers of senses unwound
& all my love painted in the clouds
To be unsober,
Another day
Liquified; skybound; delectable.

THE WAY I WALK

I've fallen in love
With the way I walk
Like an undead model
With a vengeance
I can't turn it off
But I don't mind
Anyone I pass
Is left behind
They can't keep up,
But even if they do,
They'll never own the swagger
That I do.

STRANGERS

Strangers make the strangest friends;
Making memories
To soon lose them.

THE LIVES YOU'VE KNOWN

The lives you've known
Write their own show
Of evil, serpent
Cancer cells.

VALENTINE'S DAY 2017

Sitting in a lonely bar
With lonely people
I hate.
I feel like Van Gogh.
It's alright though;
Your eyes reflect ***the*** stars

Happy Valentine's ***Day***

THE TWO: A ~~Poetry~~ Study

By Joseph Colyer

GLASS

My fingers gather ashes
& your fingers fasten around my torso

I know it not to be a sin

For we are truly fragile,
Porcelain

I find it only terrifying to think
That I've lost everything

In the bulletproof glass
Implanted behind your iris.

THE AQUARIUS I

Aquarius,
You are my only constant.

I awake in danger;
You awake in vomit.

COLLISIONS WITH NOTHING

Decorated in kisses;
Lost in the tragic
Tie-dyed constellations:
A ticket stub;
Paid admission
To this realm where we
Can fly
On angel wings
In transparent collisions
With

Nothing.

GONE

It is a rush
Of sublime beauty
Magic
Indefinite
Endless
Colors invisible to a human imagination
Energy transferred from the great beyond
To its fleshy counterparts

Gone
But the recollection.

THE TWO: A ~~Poetry~~ Study

By Joseph Colyer

PERFORMER

I'm a performer –
But I won't settle for a strip tease

I'm a romantic –
But I don't know what Love means

REALITY,

Wish you were here.

THE TWO: A ~~Poetry~~ Study

By Joseph Colyer

I CAN'T IMAGINE

I can't imagine

That the tree's branches grow heavy;

That the lotuses have trouble waking up;

That the lion's breath becomes rancid to itself;

I can only imagine,
That on the eighth day,
God left us unfinished

THE AQUARIUS II

Aquarius,
What have I done?
You are the most pure expression of Reality
Grounding me; reminding me
That I am not from stardust
I am human flesh
When our lips met
I felt no perfection,
No magical spark from the great beyond
Only the Reality
That for that brief moment
I belonged to you;
You belonged to me

I grow larger wings,
You trim them away

I offer you hope,
You hold me captive to the sun

I love everything,
You force it to fade

Aquarius,
What have I done?

SLEEPS

The City sleeps.

To what does it owe the privilege?

SNAKE

He sizes me up
Like a snake
Trying to decide
How much he can swallow.

FETAL POSITION

You sleep on the floor
In the fetal position
Like a child

Afraid to be held

N/A

Horrible poetry;
Words that make no sense
I have no voice to speak
What's vague, posionous, irrelevant
It's as if my only weapon has gone dull
& I pilot an empty skull
Prose that was once my electricity:

Limp, devoid, and null.

THE TWO: A ~~Poetry~~ Study

By Joseph Colyer

PARKING LOT

Meet me ***in the parking lot:***

Our usual spot.

We can leave behind
All the time

We'll soon think, lost.

VICTORIAN HOUSE

Victorian house;
Sweet,
Victorian house

At home in another realm
Home, when I am lost.

THE TWO: A ~~Poetry~~ Study

By Joseph Colyer

ANGER

Anger
Is a lampost
On the corner
By the bus stop
She visits in the evening
& Sometimes takes the train
She'll bare her legs,
Make you stop,
Steal your car,

& Leave you in the rain

THE WAKING HELL

Unconsciousness returns

The mind is plugged back in
Circuits misfire
The whirring of gears in desperate need
Of oil,
Elbow grease

Mechanical eyes

Pulleys pull the captive subject
From their metal bed frame
Placing their unwilling host
On a conveyer belt
To The Waking Hell

& back

GOOD POETRY

He makes for good poetry
So I keep the bag of flesh around

IN HIS HEART, LIVES THE SAME

She asked what I saw in him
I said

"Nothing"

Yet, in my heart, lives the same

Nothing

THE TWO: A ~~Poetry~~ Study

By Joseph Colyer

THE WOLVES IN SUBURBIA

I lay in bed, sick,
Like I had been with you
And, our third: Vodka

I lay in bed, awake
Like I had been in love
Infatuated with insomia

I loay in bed, disintegreated
Like I had been when you left

Me, for the wolves in suburbia

DOCTOR

"Did we play doctor"

I don't remember
But I know that you
Removed my heart
In my sleep

& SO, YOU TRANSPOSE

& so, you transpose
My feelings
Into harsh elixirs
& aromas pure

What horrible hell
Are we living for?

HAPPY

Nothing good can come from it
Nothing profound
Nothing outstanding
Nothing forlorn

Nothing from happiness
Will ever be born

THE TWO: A ~~Poetry~~ Study

By Joseph Colyer

GRASS

I wait for him
Like Chernobyl waits for chemical burns

I see him
As if under a microscope; perfectly kerned

I yearn for him
Like the forest nymph loves the fawn

I miss him
Like the grass misses being trotted upon

SUNDAY

Thursday night,
I will ruin you

Friday morning,
I will leave you

Saturday evening,
I will mourn you

Sunday,
You will confess

SERENADED BY THE SKY

Serenaded by the sky
Subtle scents of pine
Disrupted by a cigarette
Sending shivers up my spine

MY MOUTH IS A GRAVEYARD

Heaven is sweaty
My stomach is empty
My lungs are heavy
My time is spent
Baked into cakes of confetti
A weapon at ready

My mouth is a graveyard
Where dead men are sent

LONELY STALL

This place is a prison
Overcome with sickness
In this lonely stall
You don't ask permission

I KEEP WAKING UP

I keep waking up
In his bed
I hate him
Much more than I can

THE TWO: A ~~Poetry~~ Study

By Joseph Colyer

MESS

The first breath of fresh air:
Amidst gnawing into flesh:
The last taste of the dark:
This mattress is a mess

IF ALL HER LIGHT WILL FADE

She is afraid
That if she tells him
All her light will fade
That he is the spark
That tithes her reins
That he is the lark
That sings through her pain
But she is the Light
She is the King
She is the Knight
She is the Queen

THE TWO: A ~~Poetry~~ Study

By Joseph Colyer

THE VERTICAL MIRROR I

Strangers in;
Strangers out
In and out
Of this old house
Some look for drugs
Some look for hell
All of them are looking
Looking for themselves

THE VERTICAL MIRROR II

The parallel realm
Opposite side of your mirror
I want to go back
But I'm stuck here

THE VERTICAL MIRROR III

Today is strange
Nothing is the same
No communication
With the Other Side today

I can see grass aplenty
And trees becoming green
What of the Waking realm
Am I failing to see?

YOU POOR ROCKETSHIP

He is dead
We did nothiing
About the bloody tourniquets in his car
He was, but a rocketship
Out of oxygen
Lost amongst the stars

DECISIONS

Stop deciding
To dissect the decisions
That made you decide
To make those decisions.

THE VERTICAL MIRROR IV

Temporary
Five minutes of freedom
Happens so fast
I tell myself each time
That it will be the last
The joy is
Temporary
Every second in between
Bleak and randomizing

THE VERTICAL MIRROR V

Reality is a set of funhouse mirrors
Reflecting what we don't want to see
Stretching us
Stretching everything
Altering our genes

THEY WATCH ME, LIKE A CINEMA

They watch me
Like a cinema
They pull me up
On their phone
Engaging in acts,
Criminal
When they feel
That they're finally alone

THE VERTICAL MIRROR V

He keeps it dangerous
High heels,
Strangulation
& gagged conversations

If looks could kill
He's a Jacob's ladder to famous

He keeps it dangerous
He's your fixation

THE VERTICAL MIRROR VI

I find my own company
Conveniently deranged
I drag myself into Oblivion
Just staring myself in the face

CHEAP WHISKEY

You are a cheap whiskey

You get me drunk
& it doesn't feel fancy

MYSTERIOUS

He puts a cigarette behind his ear
He brings a towel outside the shower
He places me into his deepest fears
He brings mystery to every hour

THE INTERVIEW

I poured him shot after shot
& asked him a million questions
If I could understand his intentions
I could let him go
He told me of the universe
Through his eyes,
How we are made of carbon
Recycled when we die.

& that is his depression:
Reality, it would seem
Has substituted for his religion
Or any faith in the Realm in between.
I walked him back to the sunset
& waved him goodbye

To the few parts of him that I was ever allowed to see,
With a heavy heart,
I let him go

A sigh of relief.

ALWAYS BEEN THE SAME

I've run out of things to write about
My life has always been the same
And now you've read all about it

Like many,
You will forget my name

THE TWO: A ~~Poetry~~ Study

By Joseph Colyer

THE QUIET

The quiet
Is either lonely
Or incredibly liberating

But what is the difference?

LIKE WE'RE IN A CASKET

We sleep like we're in a casket
We might as well be.

My fear, is not suffocating madness
But you,
Killing me.

WHERE DOES IT GO?

For a second I felt it

That Joy,
That Spark

I wonder where it goes
When it's gone?

WHAT DELICIOUS DISAPPOINTMENT?

How distant;
How pure

What delicious disappointment?

Despair;
Awe
Disposal of the past
Until it is carefully removed
From the waste bin of memory
& its tattered pages,
Unwrinkled.

As I weep the first tears
I wish for many a sleepless night
& I wish you only well.

GOD

The lower you fall
The closer you are
To God.

THE VERTICAL MIRROR VII

People speak of losing sleep
My friends dream of psychosis

I can't help but laugh;
They don't know the half of it

THE BASEMENT

All that you hold dear
Lives in the basement.

The ideas you'll never use
The memories you abuse
The light you can't turn off at night

All below your head
Whirring, making noise
Soundless fright.

All that you hold dear
Lives in the basement.

MARRIED I

They say that
Absence
Makes the heart grow
Fonder

I'd rather die
Alone
Than be married
To a monster

THE VERTICAL MIRROR VIII

When does one come back
From the abyss?

When every smile
Is frozen?

When every path
Was already chosen?

When everything they have
Is all there is.

GHOSTS ON SWING-SETS

Now I see ghosts on swing sets
In the mountains
A Rosetta Stone preventing passage
To the summer hills
A pretentious palace
To the pearly gates
Of forbidden knowledge

THE VERTICAL MIRROR IX

This world is changing
Before my eyes
Warping;
Driving me blind.

THE VIRGIN, SCARY

Then I was the Virgin Mary
Standing beneath the chandelier
Without Frankincense
Or myrrh
No room for a bed

But I felt like gold

I felt like gold

I felt golden

Gold

Gold

Gold

THIS STRANGER'S ARMS

This stranger's arms
Feel more like home
Than yours ever did

They say all dogs go to heaven
God must love a good pig

SHOW

Pretend you're happy
Show the world you're in love
With what makes you the saddest

Show us pictures
Smiling faces
Convince your fraudulence,
Fact

TALL, DARK, & HANDSOME

He's tall;
He's dark;
He's handsome;

He's horrible.

CLASSICAL POETRY

Sex
Sells
Sex
Cells
By
The
Cheap
Whore

THE TWO: A ~~Poetry~~ Study

By Joseph Colyer

LIFE'S VHS

You're up past your bedtime
Life's VHS on rewind
Staring at the wall
Wondering how you fell behind
All your secrets tucked under your pillow
Those neat rows of teeth:
Covered, toxic yellow

And the record's on repeat

You're up past your bedtime
I think of you all the time
Staring at my reflection
Telling myself I'll be fine
All my secrets broadcast in plain sight
Scaring the bones our of others
To my sinister delight
I'll fall for another
The record always repeats
Repeats
Repeats kissing feet
Stuck grinding meat

THE PARTS THEY CAN'T SEE

A dry flaky skin
With acid flesh underneath
People are terrified
Of the parts they can't see

THE TWO: A ~~Poetry~~ Study

By Joseph Colyer

SEDATIVES I

Cold, pinhole eyes
Breathing through acid lace

Writhing bacteria
Impairing every taste

Hearing satellite imagery
From the deepest stretches
Of the darkest space

Sedatives
Really fuck up your face

WISDOM; WHAT OF IT?

God gave me ears
Not to hear
But to listen carefully

God gave me eyes
Not to see
But to witness beauty

God gave me a mouth
Not to speak
But to exhale truth

But, wisdom;
What of it?
God never gave me youth

THE TWO: A ~~Poetry~~ Study

By Joseph Colyer

THE VERTICAL MIRROR X

A demon lives, here
Behind the mirror
If you stare long enough;
He will appear
He once lived below my bed
When I was a child
But now he finds me in people
Now that I'm an adult

Who is he?
What does he want?

WHAT I DON'T WANT TO WANT

Now there is a cement wall
Between my world and yours
Protecting me from what I don't want to want
Guardian angels keep me safe
From defeats I don't deserve
But my heart still overflows
With the strongest lust I've ever known.

Oh, Love, be still.

THERE'S SOMETHING WRONG

There's something wrong
About eating alone
There's something wrong
About not eating at all

There's something wrong
About sleeping alone
There's something wrong
About not sleeping at all

There's something wrong
About smoking alone

There's something wrong
I smoke way too much.

RIBCAGE

I can see my ribcage
I can see the sharp blade
Daggers in your shoulder blades

I can't tell if my vertebrae
Are all fused together

I can see her eyes fade
I can see her heart race
Crying in the shower

Store my body in a safe place
You'll feel better someday

EVERYONE I KNOW IS AN ARTIST

Everyone I know is an artist
The construction worker
The fortune teller
The pastry chef
The mechanic

YET, NOT ENOUGH

I am surrounded by guilt
An air of acceptance
Melancholy sounds
Slow motion
Stop and go
Traffic lights
& Silent filth
That you can hear if you listen close
To see the lights
So much shame
Yet, not enough

YOU NEED AFFECTION

Wait for the buzz
Wait for the Love
You need affection
You need your drugs

BEHIND CLOSED DOORS

At what point
Did my heart say
        "It's hot when he punches
        Holes
        Through the wall?"

There's shock value
In the disgust you can't recall
Easier if
We don't feel
Pain or joy at all

& at what point
Did my heart say
        "Go back for more"
History happens
Behind closed doors

ONLY HOPE

I can only hope
To love another
We spoke
But never uttered
A single word

THIS IS THE WAY

This is the way
The world ends
Not with a bang,
But with
A brain tumor

A BED SHEET

I am poison through a straw
A bathroom covered in shit
An abandoned shopping mall
A bed sheet stained with shit

IN PUDDLES

The past laughs at you
In puddles on the sidewalk
Trying to look like you
Exasperated smalltalk
Hands all over you
Squeezing lemons
Drop
By
Drop
In order to outrun you
Must first know how to walk

TWENTY-TWO YEARS

Twenty-two years
I've spent in the body
Of a recycled soul
Sent to planet earth
With extraterrestrial
Cosmic memories
From some other
Time or space
I have spent nine lives
Somewhere else
& they come back
In flashes
I know that they come in peace
But what could they possibly mean?

RESTRICTING ALL RISK

Open relationship;
Why deal with the shit?
For freedom of body;
Or freedom of filth?

Monogamous relationship;
Why deal with the shit?
Loving only in Siamese;
Restricting all risk?

MEMORIES OF PSEUDO-FAUX I

Long
Lost
Love
Long
Gone
Before
I
Leave
Tell
Me
Everything
We
Had
Yet
To
Do
I
Can't
Love
You
You
Can't
Love
Anything

APRIL SHOWERS

The sky: a blue hue
The ashes: residue
The dawn of a new hour:

April showers
May bring back my powers

THE TWO: A ~~Poetry~~ Study

By Joseph Colyer

LIFE IMITATES

Life
Imitates
Life
Imitates
Life
Imitates
Life
Imitates
Life
Imitates
Life
Imitates
Life
Imitates
Life
Imitates
Life
Imitates
Life
Imitates
Life
Imitates
Life

MEMORIES OF PSEUDO-FAUX II

The basement
The white rug
The kisses
The backrubs
The moans
The screams
The everything in between
The horrible dreams
The tightrope
The sunsets
Over
The crime scene
You pressing too fard
        Too hard
        To leave

D.A. / D.A.

Like cracks
In dry sand
We wander
Across a desert
& an ocean of mirages
Burying our treasures
When we can
She carries me
To this dry land

Oh,

What a pleasure
To be in the presence
Of such a Goddess

WHEN YOU'RE DONE

Babe, when you're done
Throwing up
You can come to bed
I never did
& woke up next to a plate of dead bread

THE TWO: A ~~Poetry~~ Study

By Joseph Colyer

I, MELT

Top bunk
To ourselves
The room perfumed
With gasoline

Covered couch
I, melt
When you
Touch anything

THE VERTICAL MIRROR XI

I've been here before
This place where the walls cave in
& she has seven eyes

The rumors are all true

My hands trace
In and out of time
The floor is quicksand
Decorated in jagged blades
With all the edges softened
It's always a treat
I love it here.

Yes, I come here often.

SWEEPSTAKES

You've won a vacation!

Congratulations!

A sweepstakes
To a desert island
Where ice crystallizes
Over violence
& paradise
Is dreadful silence
We celebrate
At your compliance
Some would call it luck

But, mindless.

FOR TOO LONG

It happened
For far too long
& then it was
Too far gone

THE TWO: A ~~Poetry~~ Study

By Joseph Colyer

EMBRACE

finalebastile
fighttofeel
embracedecay
erasethederanged
nospaceremains
poetryissostrange

CORNER

Sitting in the corner
Waiting on the coroner
The doctors say that Karma
Has passed away

DEAD ROSES ON THE COUNTER

There is idle chatter
& tables of liquor
Dead roses on the counter
Unwelcome visitors
Smoke
Fills our lungs
Songs are sung
Out of tune
We think of all the lives
That we could all but ruin
Everyone's asking question
But I don't know the answers
Dead roses on the counter
& much welcome cancers

IT IS NOT TRUE

It is not true
Air,
I don't breathe quite the same
As you

THE VERTICAL MIRROR XII

I make love
To a silver screen
In this other Realm
Where hearts go to scream
Nothing here
Is as you could have possibly dreamed

Ripped to shreads, the astral seams

IF I WROTE ABOUT YOU

If I wrote about you
You would know

You would feel it
In your bones
Like I feel
Your empty soul
The brick and mortar
Between my toes

I see each day

You walk a tightrope
If I wrote about you
You would know

By Joseph Colyer

NINE BOXES

Nine boxes cover the screen
Their contents:
Bodies belonging
To souls you'll never meet
The sky is falling
But we find solace
In this culture composed
Of subcultural madness

HOUSE

We play house
But no one is home

MARRIED II

Police
At my door
Candles
Burn
Into a liquid
Fairy dust
Takes
You to the forest
To your own
Prison
Snorting
Pixie sticks
Off my uncircumcision
This is not
The marriage
I had envisioned

I LOVE HIM (LIKE A BROTHER)

He's just a friend
I love him like a brother
Of his kind,
I've met no other
He sleeps like an angel
With the soul of a child

But he's just a friend

By Joseph Colyer

IN HALF A MILE

In half a mile
Turn right onto
West fourth street
Where the smiles
Turn to defeat
Where the styles
Are monotony
And inspiration
Comes at a bleak
Price to pay

STRANGE?

Strange to look closer?
Strange to denounce danger?
Strange to seek questions
That lead to less answers?

THE TWO: A ~~Poetry~~ Study

By Joseph Colyer

WE ARE TWO

We are Two
Halves
Torn apart
Winning a race
That never
Starts
We fall
From grace
Salvaging the spare parts
Our ego is
Larger
Than our hearts

Will ever be again

DRAW A TRIANGLE

Draw a triangle

In that triangle
Place a vase

Fill it with hate
And resentment
Cast away the crowds
With mace

Now bury it in a lake
Like a corpse
Lost at sea

Forget all the lives
Your eyes
Were never meant to see

YOU CAN LEAD A HORSE TO WATER

You can lead a horse to water
But you cannot make it drink
You can teach a man to follow
But never how to think

THE TOP OF THE MOUNTAIN

Collosal disappointment
The top of the mountain
Is never quite the top
Unrealistic expectations
Always chasing the dragon

THE TWO: A ~~Poetry~~ Study

By Joseph Colyer

I NEVER KNOW WHAT TO DO WITH MY HANDS

I never know what to do with my hands

Do I pose like a puppet?
Do I gesture in the dark?
Do I hold the cigarette?
Do my nails leave marks?

I'll never know what to do with my hands

SOMEHOW

Somehow
I'm still

TOMORROW NIGHT

All inspiration drained
Replaced with heat
Strokes
Kerosene
On an empty stomach
Pulls
On my heart strings
Pools
Of vomit

Tomorrow night
Is Haley's comet

VEINS; ARTERIES

An owl turns its head
Full round
We use our ears
Only to hear sound
We colonize as if
Underground
Our veins
Our arteries
Tied to the clouds

THE TWO: A ~~Poetry~~ Study

By Joseph Colyer

EARTH

I am feeling things
I have never felt before
Not feelings for you
But for Planet

Earth

BIRTH

A dot in space
They call the Earth
Such a gamble with fate
That we gave

Birth

To what the galaxy
Has never seen before
And likely will
Never see again

UNCOMPARABLE BEAUTY

I can't compare beauty
To any other sight

Yes, I buy roses
So I can watch them die

YOU HAVE TO BREATHE

You have to breathe

No writing
No art
No painting
No poetry
No love

The irony
Of it all

MARRIED III

There's pornography
On the TV
Dirty dishes
In the sink
This is not like
In the movies
The entire apartment
Stinks
Of sorrow;
Humiliation

SHAMOKIN, PA

Shamokin
Where the dead
Come to die
They say you can find LSD
If I don't mind mining
With my eyes

ATOMIC BLOND

My heart was an atom bomb
Nuclear fission
Of spiky red blood cells
Beating as frequent
As the beatings
Slow, intense
Keeping me alive

BEHIND THE BULLETPROOF GLASS

I saw your face behind the glass
A prisoner
With a chiseled chin
"What's in it for me"
I asked he

Truly, a prison, as well.
Or a palace, no other will see

CALM ICE

When I met you
It was the calm
Before the storm

Now that you're gone
It is but ice
To a burn

A MOST TERRIFYING NIGHT

The value of the grey
In the ceiling
Slowly raises to white
As the sun rises
Behind the blinds

It's been a most terrifying night

There are faint glows from the hallway
But not a single soul
I am in this house alone
Listening with precaution
To my own heart beating
As if, a mile away

MY PSYCHE DOES NOT BRUISE

You find amuse
In using others

So my psyche does not bruise
When I am using you

CLIENT

A weekly allowance
At my compliance
Unlimited stones
If I'll be your client
If you asked me before
I don't do that anymore

I'll pay you in gold
If you leave me alone

BIPOLAR DISORDER

Bipolar disorder
You reek of disorder
The gems in your teeth
'Cause you think you're a martyr
For a cause that's not your own
Crafting yourself a throne
Of sadness or wealth
Dependent of the hour
You'll understand
When you're older

If you live that long

MEMORIES OF PSEUDO-FAUX III

Stay
The
Night
If
You
Like
We
Won't
Fight
Our
Hands
Are
Cut
It's
Not
Right
But
Our
Hands
Are
Cut
With
Extreme
Precision
Our hands are cut

THE TWO: A ~~Poetry~~ Study

By Joseph Colyer

WASP

I am a wasp
My own acid
Turns me sour
Hurting
My tail stings
To a ballad
Known only fiends of flowers
And the pretentious song birds
Keep singing louder

THE VERTICAL MIRROR XIII

I never wanted forever here
I didn't ask for
'Till death do us part
But forever found me
In the dotted lines
Etched around the door
To the Realm
Within the sky
It begged
        "Cut here"
Then
        "Enter at your own risk"
& followed quickly
With warning signs
        "Private property;
        Trespassers will be prosecuted"
I never asked for forever
But I got what I asked for

CHEAP COLONS

Cheap:
Hearts:
Hung:
On the clearance rack
Colons:
On a blown:
Out sale

ABOMINATION

The sound of gunpowder
Reverberates off the backs of the pupils
Cloaked, bulletproof glass
All the colors of the rainbow, darling
Hidden in plain sight
Reflecting fireworks,
The illusion of class

Gone up in marijuana smoke
In the night

THE TWO: A ~~Poetry~~ Study

By Joseph Colyer

THE TIME IT TAKES

Deprivation: no sleeping
Everything is vague
The time it takes
To write it all down
Has made minutes
Deem themselves days

LOVE IS

Love is camouflaged
To stand out
Love is the wind
Beneath the wings of birds

FIVE MILLION + FIVE

Five million
Plus five
What happens when we die?
Do we have to stay here?
Do we live in the sky?
Is life any better when we're alive?
The possibilities; the mistakes
I created them; they're mine.

Yours are yours too
Five million
Plus five

YOU BUY ME A DRINK

You buy me a drink
You ask where I'm from
Who cares what I think?
You just want to cum

THE TWO: A ~~Poetry~~ Study

By Joseph Colyer

CREATURE

Moving through the cemetery
I saw a bright light
Fly into the sun
In its place stood a figure
Standing upright
With jaws made to bite
With a tongue
Made of spite
Running like smoke,
It needn't not move
It made its way across the tombs
Crawling, the creature ventured
At the speed of fright
Sidled up to my bedside,
Glaring into my eyes,
Strangling me
With a smile
With its metal spikes
In place of a spine

It whispered in my ear
Words I could hear
Clear as Sunday morning:

"No darling,
Not tonight
Perhaps in another life
You'll join me here:
Where shadows hide
Fulfilling your wish
To be out of sight"

I could not decipher
What I've witnessed:
A warning
Or a charming

It suffocated me one last time
With those beautiful baby brown eyes
Before evaporating
Into the grave gravity of the night

PREDICTABLE UNPREDICTABILITY

Maybe we'll do the deed
Perhaps we'll watch the TV
We waste all of our time
In predictable unpredictability

STAPLED

God stapled
My eyelids open
He put a bullet
Between my lips
Most live
Their lives hoping
They could ever
Taste a kiss as this

THE TWO: A ~~Poetry~~ Study

By Joseph Colyer

THE MEMORY

He poses: statuesque,
In a grounded grandeur;
Planting daffodils in fields
That he always fails to see.

He is majesty:
Beautiful and grotesque
When he touches me,
I can hardly breathe

Yet, here in his arms,
I know I'm far from free;
For the memory is fonder
Than the reality will ever be

REMEMBERING

There are knives in the ceiling
A kitchen table in the bed
A door to where the walls meet
Where you've locked away the meds

Yet, this is not a nightmare
It's not in your head
You are simply remembering
Please, go back to bed

THE OCEAN

If she slipped into the light fixture,
Would anyone miss her?

Would the witches wonder,
What potions could have fixed her?

Endless fascinations,
With her nighttime mixtures
& translucence under
Waterbed masturbation

How could you love her
With all her bones fractured?

If she dove into the ocean,
Would anyone find her?

IN TRUTH

In truth,
He is the only soul I've ever written for

The boy was always him
The Love was always ours

THAT WAS ALL TOO REAL

I let the day take over me
Too many nights had fallen
& too many knights had slain
My dragons before

Like a waterfall of profanity,
I allowed the hallucinations to come as the would

I saw a dead child take the form of a deer
I saw it rear its horned head in fear
& saunter away from me, quickly

I saw the nighttime in evaporation
I saw Love notes and pleas for help
Drawn in the condensation

I saw people walking the earth like zombified corpses

But that was all too real

THE COST OF TOMORROWS

Stolkholm Syndrome
Is a funny thing
First a snow cone
Then he's your everything
They'll downplay your sorrows
Crown her a king
Fashion her a throne
& cut away your wings
But inside this dome
Made of flesh
& thin bone
Beats an organ
That will cost you tomorrows
Far more
Than searching
For what any
A fickle human heart
Could possibly
Have thoughts to fathom

THE TWO: A ~~Poetry~~ Study

By Joseph Colyer

I WOKE UP UNDER A TREE

I woke up under a tree
In the forest
I cried and made
Quiet contact
With that second space
Under the old wooden swing set
Wind chimes
Do not make music
They make confetions
& treehouses are not homes
But I could grow roots
In this tired tree
My soul is exhausted
So I walk the tightrope
Across the chasm
Shouting
"I love you" into the void
But, like the Spanish film,
The dark space doesn't elicit a response
Echoed back
Instead I hear
Rustling
In the decaying leaves around me

& I know it to be the same
Sounds
That come when you throw
A coin into a wishing well
Only to wish your enemies well
At the bottom of this well
I feel concrete pressed against
My chin
& my missing teeth
I have long ago removed
Scattered around me
Like the crime scene in the bathroom
Like medical gloves
Stretched for a procedure
That can always prove fatal

THE TWO: A ~~Poetry~~ Study

By Joseph Colyer

AS LOVELY

I was but one
But one of three
Under the trees
Of evergreen
Castles protected
The terrible scene
&, of the three
I was their queen
He was weak
So was she
Neither they,
Nor the scene
Quite as lovely
As me

CANDID CORPSE OF A DOVE

Such power, rightfully earned
In her strength, She saves,
The candid corpse of a dove
She perches Herself, a Beacon
& angels gather above
Like a river, Magic runs
Where her feet meet the Earth,
She exhales carbon
& inhales Love
She is a goddess,
Brighter, more deadly, than the sun
You are Her:
The Heiress to the Chosen One

ON DELUSIONS OF GRANDEUR

My delusions of grandeur
Are not delusions at all

For, I have come to understand
If we can think ourselves
Indestructible
Than indestructible
We are

SEDATIVES II

Sedation
Is a frigid slap in the face
After a holiday
Gone south

Sedation
Is the sweet caress
Of numbness
In your mouth

Sedation
Is great for your mind
But bad
For your health

Sedation
Sells so fast
That they can't keep it
On the shelves

YOU ARE NOT AN ARTIST

Everyone is an artist
If you think that art
Is reserved for artists
Than you, my dearest
Are not an artist

ETHAN

You were a lovely stranger
Rum and coke
& a signature
Signed "Danger"
I didn't know you
But now you know me
Perhaps coincidence
But I foresee destiny
Dearest tall man
With hair like night
You have been the highlight
Of my entire life

A SINGLE TEAR

A single tear rolls down my cheek
I have to rub my eyes
To stop myself from seeing
The living memory standing in front of me

TRUE

I always perform
To an empty room
Of brain stems
Who care not for you

Save for sometimes: one
On the lucky nights: two

An active scandal:
The rumors, true.

THE TWO: A ~~Poetry~~ Study

By Joseph Colyer

BLUEGREEN

Painted in blue
Across the green:
Two worlds that
No longer meet
One is cold,
The other: unseen
My soul is a parted sea.

HER

I have never known
A heart as hers

Every t-shirt,
An evening gown
That men seem to
Adore

But I have known
Many hearts as hers

Constant rebirth
Hidden under a crown
A smile, Medusa made of
Stone
A pressure made to
Perform

G.A.G.A.

Meaty fabric
Coarse & thick
Sewn together
Black magic
The model walks
Tall and straight
You'll meet her
On the news
The very next day

AMETHYST

Diamonds tile the floor
My ass is an amethyst
A dodecahedron heart
Sliced into rubies

The road to hell
Is paved with gold
Good intention
Decorates its doors

SCARED TO LEAVE THE RECTANGLE

I am scared to leave the rectangle
That keeps us safe
Where time can not touch us
& we don't count the days
The air outside strangles
In this shape, we remain violent
Love is all we need
I'm not moving forward
That's final
The quilt is soft
& you are hard to the touch

DESOLATE

I watched the water lap against my feet
& thought "I hope I remember this"
In your heart,
I saw a playground
Desolate
I watched you drive my car
Into a storm
By my side in the sand
The space where I once saw angels
Their spot, now you've taken
In a roach motel label "vacant"
& now I inhabit,
What I meant for you: a throne
I looked across the world
& I saw you

Walking through the forest,
Alone

FOREST

It is tattooed upon our stars
Everything that ever would be
Everything that ever was
It predicted all our scars
Everything you told me

When I touched the dead ferns in the forests

HAPPINESS IN ARABIC

You type letters to me
Written backwards

You share your love with me
In the form of records

Repeating all the time

THE DICHOTOMY OF OURSELVES

A book placed on the shelf
A collection of divine

Ice cream always melts
Gastric acid lines our insides

The cave in which the monsters dwell
Is decorated with lies written by the mind

The dichotomy of ourselves
Eats itself alive

COMMANDO

He returned my clothes
I’ve missed them so
How does anyone live like this
He had my favorite pair of underwear

I’ve gone commando ever since

THE VERTICAL MIRROR XIV

I hear white noise
In the room next to the sun

I know it's you

The angel in my body: numb
My psyche: subdued
I yearn to exchange
Worlds with you
The only color
Here is Black

& all your goo
Seeps through

THE DARK SPOT OF JUPITER

He is
The dark spot of Jupiter,
The cold of Pluto's dark,
The sound of Saturn's rings;
He is my everything;
An angel whom lost his wings,
To pour lead into his heart

But how could he know;
By littering my neck in marks,
He's filled my empty spaces
Like the Heaven he'll never see?

THE SAD TREE

I don't remember much
About where I used to be
Except for outside my house
Stood a lonely tree
Its branches: always dead
It swayed, as if it weeped
At night, when I stumbled home
Terrified, I'd be
I expected it to come alive
As I fumbled for the keys
& dropped pieces
Of shards of glass
Mangled at my feet
For, if I wandered too close
Near that sad tree
I feared I'd see
The likes of which
No soul's ever seen

IF ONLY HUMANS KNEW

If only humans knew
That Love is not a fairytale
A destination to pursue
Love is simply the universe
That lives inside of you
The fabric of space
A sacred intention
God's truest face:
A divine intervention
To shed the ego,
To place ourselves second
To alleviate which suffers
Of ourselves:

The fourth dimension

Is at our command,
If we only payed it attention;

Love is not a destination

MARRIED IV

I slice myself on thorns
To smell that one, sacred rose

I solidify a fortress
Inside the walls of vacant hotels

I pay passage to secrets
I can't fathom words to tell

I am a body
Without the demand to sell

I empty my wallet
Into every wishing well

I'll marry you
But, in Love, you never fell

For that single flickering Light,
I suffer through hell

You'll think I wrote you this,
For you think only of yourself

PERMANENT

You are at the tip of my pen
I can't get you out

You bleed that mustard color
Into even the blackest of ink

You must be permanent,
So I let you stay in the tip of my pen

You make the paper a bloody mess,
But I love you anyway

Even the mistakes we make together
On the page, seem important

God, I wish
You were permanent

BEDROOMS ARE OUR CHURCHES

Every bedroom
Is a place of projection
Where a soul goes to rest
& seek protection

When you enter someone else's
Divine dimension
You will often find a heart
Absent of direction,
In need of guidance,
In need of distraction,
All without a person,
To assume the position

SHE IS EVERYTHING

She deserves the solar system;
You gave her space dust

She is alive with electricity;
You pulled the plug

She is a cosmic collision;
You reduced her, numb

She is everything – You are the opposite
You are not worthy of her love

ARTIFICIAL NOSTALGIA

I used to think that my parents' world
Existed only in black and white
Because it looked that way in the photos

I used to think that music
Was rock & roll
Because that's what I heard on my Walkman

I used to think that the world
Was in the palm of my hands
Because I was always told that I was special

Now I know, it's not so at all;
We are either nostalgic and artificial

DON'T

Don't tell me your name

Don't show me your face

I won't remember you;
Won't remember your place

That's how it must be
This story will remain the same

How hard could it be?
Please,

Don't.

Tell me your name.

SEND

We write messages with our bodies
That we never can decide to send

THE VERTICAL MIRROR XV

Gravity
Pulls you closer to the core
He is just
The boy next door
We sleep on
Separate bathroom floors
Out of portals
Back to the Other world.
In Your Vertical Mirror,
I yearn for you

HANDFUL

Nothing on the airwaves,
A handful of heart-shaped pills
At the break of day

PUT IT AWAY

I hear I'll have to grow up someday:

Put my love and toys away

Yet, perhaps they have no words to say,
That they fear the fear they hold so dear
Be willed to evaporate
By He who has no Heart to break

CTHULHU

Chances are, I frighten you
For, in my voice, lives Cthulhu

I stand for the Unknown
& all that ails you

I am the god
That never fails you

WISH

We all have that one wish
We wish we didn't miss:
That cherry ember,
His cherry lips,
Snowy November,
Two years: spent sick

STALE

I have grown stale as the bread once left
Beside my sleeping body

WASTE-BIN

I sang to you
At your bedside
You look
Positively divine
Our hearts combined
Our atoms divided
& now I look by my side
& see you
Pale as a ghost
In a room coated, caked with smoke
Beside a waste-bin, littered in puke

MARRIED V

He is my subsidiary:
Filament in the landfills of my body
He is Beta,
He kisses my feet
While church bells ring in marriage
To precursors
To this sex they have yet to meet

WHAT WOULD HAPPEN?

What would happen
If I let you go
Would it render null
Every poem
I ever wrote?

THE TWO: A ~~Poetry~~ Study

By Joseph Colyer

BATTLE

A civil war:
Our hearts at battle
I could never love the battle
As much as I love you

You could never love me
As much as you love the bottle

TWO BETAS

Two betas
In a fish bowl
They say we'll eat eachother
Whole

But to what do we owe this
Feeding frenzy of competition?
We both bear plumes
Like peacocks in submission

But my feathers bleed colors
Into the water;
Even if
I end up
In his stomach
There was never any contest

I grow more colorful by the second

SHE'S DRIVING ME INSANE

She is untampered energy:
An atom bomb
On the astral plane
She drives me insane
But I love her

The same

BUSINESS, BABY

Coins rattle in my tube-socks;
I don't get paid nearly enough

Can't breathe a word, till the tape is off;
It's just business, baby

Money talks.

VISUALIZATION MEDITATION

A gust of wind, that you can't see
A sunbeam through broken blinds
An analog clock with deceased batteries
A flawless smile, in no way kind

A skinny vixen with clogged arteries

TUNNEL VISION

I awoke to chapped lips
In an empty room, waiting for answers

Did you even ask
Permission?

I stumble,
Like a slinky down the stairway banister

The latest fashion: Cancer
Heard it from a friend: is it in Remission?

You nourish me with oil -
Feed it to me through a funnel

Is there a light at the end of this tunnel
Vision?

THE TWO: A ~~Poetry~~ Study

By Joseph Colyer

NEUTRAL

I conceive words
That come out smoother
Than the time
I had said was last
But you, as usual,

Remain neutral

Not my future, nor my past

CONVERSATION I

"I want to leave everything behind
When I go
So my memories can't define my worth"

"Don't you want to remember
Where you came from?"

"...Dirt?"

LUST IS A BATTLEFIELD

I'll meet you on the battlefield tomorrow
The final frontier
In our little uncivil war
The last nails in the coffin,
To our little love affair

I'll meet you on the battlefield tomorrow
But this final time, I won't play fair

Won't play in your hair
Won't kiss you everywhere
All truth
If you dare

The final sight you'll see of me
Will be with your legs in the air

FORK

Your body
Makes my cake crumble

You devour my crumbs
With a fork

DOUBLE-BARRELED

Your nipples are double-barreled
Bruising my chest
Mint condition; handsome,
But oh, the holes that you've left

I DON'T KNOW

I don't know
What I'm going to do without you

MEMORIES OF PSEUDO-FAUX IV

Drugs
Fights
Party
Lights
What's
The
Use
Of
Living
Right
When
Everyone
Around
You
Leaves
The
Light
?

RINGS

My skull rings with images
Of the night before
& all the days we planned
That never quite

Ever
Were

THE TWO: A ~~Poetry~~ Study

By Joseph Colyer

FATHER

Blueberries

Water

Like son,
Like father

WASTED

I will remember this room
The room where I always sit

Waiting

Candles,
Roses,
Bottle,
Smoke

Yet, here I always sit

As wasted as my time.

THE TWO: A ~~Poetry~~ Study

By Joseph Colyer

STICK-Y

Sticky hands
Sticky nightstand
Sticky,
      Sticky,
            Sticky

Stick-figure man

SEASONS CHANGE

By day, we Fall weary
Distant, frigid as Winter
By night, we Spring awake
Blinded by the sunshine of Summer

THE VERTICAL MIRROR XVI

As the sand
Fills the bottom portion
Of the hourglass,
The Waking Realm

Grows

Nearer.

STOLKHOLM CHEF

He cooks for me
So I am not worthy

Of all the love
He always shows me

CONVERSATION II

"She was abusive."

"Aren't we all?"

RIDDLES & POEMS

You speak in riddles

I speak in poems

It is unlikely that we would ever succeed
In communicating

Thank God,
We both kiss with tongue

PISSING CONTEST

How do you win a pissing contest?
Keep it in your pants

LOVESICK

Condoms in the waste-basket;
I'm staring at the ceiling

Some have called me Lovesick;
But I find this dilemma most musing

THE TWO: A ~~Poetry~~ Study

By Joseph Colyer

DO YOU LOVE HER?

She dances in the moonlight
Like sunshine
She is warm

"Do you love her?"

I ask
& he says yes

But the roses
She had sewn
Around his heart
Proved to be in decay
His skin
Was like ice
His eyes
Were frozen over

"Oh, how familiar!"

So I plucked the deceased flowers
& tossed them carelessly
Into a casket

Lowered six feet under
Marked by a headstone
Engraved

"HOMEWRECKER"

I, LOVE

I love
Like an imploding star

By the time my light reaches you,
I will be gone

WHAT TO DO WITH MY HANDS?

I'd love to let you go,
But my hands are tied

THE TWO: A ~~Poetry~~ Study

By Joseph Colyer

SPRING

Now the Spring is over
The sun is out
Now, the nightmare has ended
& I am without
He who had made
The summer so vibrant before

ACCIDENT

I am the worst
Accident
You've ever seen

Terrifying,
But you keep your eyes
Dead-set on me

SO HE WAITS

So, he waits

So, he writes

WHAT YOU NEVER COULD

We sleep in our clothes
All our hatred, transposed

We stumble through the day
As if nobody knows
About where we go

At the end of the day,
Two stubborn souls
Too afraid
To be gay

Yet, through the portals we go;
I start the show

& your eyes say
What you never could

FAUVIST FRIENDS

& though it was not of their realm,
They stood outside when I smoked
& loved me the most
When I was broken

THE VERTICAL MIRROR XVII

Mirror, mirror,
I'm too far gone

Show me your secrets
& I'll show you mine

PREVIOUS HEARTS

He reminds you of me
Reminds you of him
Reminds you of her

We swoon
For all of the hearts we've already adored

VOYEUR

It's a real-life Brokeback Mountain
A love: forbidden
& not a lot in common
A voyeuristic photograph
Vignette edges

Softened

"How have you been?"

"Do you come here often"

RENEWED

Keep me from seeing stars
From seeing the signs
Of dollars
From feeling
Like a model

They say no risk of abuse

We're all obsessed with bottles
But mine always needs renewed
Side effects may include
"What the hell is wrong with you?"

DEAR MANIA,

I adore you

You make me feel
Like the most handsome person in the room
You give me endless ideas,
Happy thoughts,
A heart full of butterflies

But when you go,
It drains the color from my eyes

You tell me I can have anyone I want
I believe you

But you make me feel so special
I could love none as you

Though the last time we sat down for a meal
All we shared was a single bottle of peppermint liquor

The absence of nutrition only makes the appeal
That much more real

Hopefully, you'll stick around,
Yours truly,
Joseph

THE TWO: A ~~Poetry~~ Study

By Joseph Colyer

YOUR CRYPT

Your body is a graveyard,
That spirits linger in at night
I would have changed the course
Of history
If only to excavate your tomb

But when I entered your Crypt

I found messages in red
        "Leave
        Get out
        Turn back now"
But I could not
The door had already closed
& I saw your corpse covered in
Maggots, sewage, and letters of admiration from him
& now I chronicle the time spent in this iron room
It feels as though I am shackled to the stones
His spirits have lifted me to
In some small way
I try to make conversation
Small talk
But the sound of you decomposing

Is the only response you elicit
Yet that is enough for me
Least I have another soul trapped
Here, too
Here, two

THE VERTICAL MIRROR XVIII

I have cast a portal in the vertical mirror
You can look,
But can't touch
The invitation is open, my dear
& you
Are finally receptive
To the Good Dark

Step through to me
On the Other Side
Play with me
In the place of our youth,
Where our shadows hide
Where our souls divide
& Lust is all we know

There is not much to fear
What are we to lose?

Our hearts?
Hah!
Pay them no mind.

Yours was always black
Mine was always blue

THE TAKEAWAY

Everyone I know
Has once mentioned to me
That they wanted to die

Oh, what a beautiful time
In history
To be

Alive

Or not to be?

BEFORE

Love was two hands fastened around my neck

Four limbs bound to bricks of cement

CHANGE

Change is the only thing
That ever stays

Change yourself
To find your Way

SOLACE

You'll see my paintings when you sleep,
You'll hear my poetry when you awake,

All though you'll lie with another
That another is no longer me

And that is solace enough

CONVERSATION III

"You were either buying cocaine
Or sleeping with him."

"Which is worse?"

TUESDAY MORNING

You have a different girl
For every day of the week
Like a twisted medication lineup
For an elderly soul

I need a sedative
Just to watch you
Down your cocktail of pills
With Hennessy

& address me by my generic name:
Tuesday Morning

WHAT AM I TO DO NOW?

He takes pills that are blue
But I'd rather the red

All things I've penned
Have come from his bed

He's one of few men
I can't get out of my head

So, what am I to do now
Without him?

I LOVE YOU

I love you
I loathe you

I wish I'd never known you

LOVING YOU IS

A hangover

6:22

Closure came at 6:22
In daylight, not night

There were no more secrets to hide
No police sirens;
No gun fights
Just silence

At 6:22

I returned home
Sedated; confused

Removed of all presence
At 6:22

IF WHAT HAPPENED ALREADY HAPPENED

If the sky bleeds multicolored oil,
How am I to see the stars?

If the Earth is so unforgivably beautiful,
Why do I dream of life on Mars?

If my heart is a loudspeaker,
Why do I only hear the echoes?

If what happened already happened,
Why can't I let it go?

DEAREST MUSE OF MY ART,

I've loved so many hearts;
& I will love so many more
Just know, of all the hearts
I've yet to travel to,
& of all those
I've already adored,
My favorite one,
So far, by far was

Yours

Truly,
Joseph

WINGS

I asked him if I was safe.
        I was met with dead air.

I said "Between our souls, sleeps gunpowder"
        At the stars, he simply stared.

I told him "I am an angel"
        He told me "Your wings are bent."

He placed my kaleidoscope to his face
        & finally understood what I meant.

INEVITABLY

Would you have seen me differently,
If you didn't know that how you loved me

Would inevitably
Be
Poetry

THE TWO: A ~~Poetry~~ Study

By Joseph Colyer

FAMOUS

I

Feel famous every day

SLOPPY SECONDS

Sloppy seconds
All it took was a second
To turn your body
Into a weapon
A metal pipe
Caked in resin
& mountains of cocaine:
Cheaper by the dozen

STELLAR

You sit in a bed of neon,
Where I have found a palace
Of prismatic colors

All I know
Is from beyond Pluto,
Earth appears to be ultraviolet

I find my only pleasure in space;
It is the only forever

My blood runs cold

Such stellar Silence

ZIP

I sit in a silent room
Silent, after the winds
Finally slammed the door shut
That I had left open

Now, zip your lips
Shackle shut the locks
Incinerate the locket

Return the damned key

STARVING

I've lost my appetite

For you

GLASS HOUSE

Melancholia will see you
Through the walls
Of your glass house

PARTY TRICK

You bite your lip:
Your party trick

I bite my tongue:
& do the bare minimum

OATH

We took an oath
To never care for each other

& formed a bond
That will last forever

THE TWO: A ~~Poetry~~ Study

By Joseph Colyer

ART:

(Noun)
The study of distilling the human experience

QUENCH

I pour him another drink
To quench his thirst
It's like water torture
But ten times worse

THE TWO: A ~~Poetry~~ Study

By Joseph Colyer

FAMILY

You sharpen your nails on me;
We call ourselves family

I walk with a rose in my
Teeth in place of thorns
You sit with a dagger
Attached to the couch,
& I am skewered
Surrounded by wealth

I would sell it all,
If only I could announce
That I am the Fire
That, in the Fall,
Migrates South

CONVERSATION IV

"You need to get out if you ever want to get out"

SCARLET LETTERED

When I awoke on the operating table,
& finally got a look at everything,
It was as if I wasn't born with twigs for arms,
Two worthless gemstones for eyes,
& a heart blazed with

Scarlet:
Lettered in calligraphy

BLINDS

Freedom didn't come
At 6:22
A.M.
It came when the Light bled between
The Blinds: painting the air an aura
Iridescent & Alien

I NEVER KNOW

You always stare
At the floor as I walk out,
So you don't have to watch
My fair skin decompose
Back from your lover,
To a mere friend.

I'm sure to collect all of my belongings
Before I turn to go;

I never know if I'll ever see you again.

OPEN HEART

The stars did not choose you
To speak themselves through
Your hands cannot dance
As mine do
God stitched your body free
Of a thousand open wounds,

Lest He never left you with an Open Heart

STORIES

They never fail to erect
Statues
For any cause, for any
Martyr
Time tells that
Stories
Often outlive their
Authors

KARMA

Why can't I sleep tonight?
Is it the mania, or the trauma?
The cigarettes, or the ganja?

My curse, or my karma?

PICTURE

Take...

A picture; I always last

...Longer

KINGS & QUEENS

Water off trees,
Falling from bliss,
Opalescent daydreams,
& temporal splits
The powers that be
Want us to see
That the world seems
A myriad more than this;
The universe is full
Of kings and queens

THE TWO: A ~~Poetry~~ Study

By Joseph Colyer

FICTION

Truth is my addiction
I simply can't write fiction

FLOWERS

Flowers from me didn't represent
"I love you; always"

They were an acknowledgment
That the spark generated
By our two hearts intertwined,
Like all things on this planet,
Will eventually die

I handed them to you in a pitcher
So you'd have a container
For something strong to wash down
The sweet and sour taste,
I left in your mouth

& you could move on with your life

As if I didn't know that night,
What I know now

THE VERTICAL MIRROR XIX

The quiet insanity of being alone:
To meet yourself in your own reflection,
The muffling of conversational sound,
The stifling of electronic noise

A throne of thorns and endless afternoons
Surrounded by your own possessions
With no hearts around
To hold dear

MARKS

I will start to disregard
The marks on your neck

If you promise to pretend
Not to see the ones on me

DREAMS I CAN RECALL

My grandfather owns a palace
In the sky, among the peasants
We crouch behind the picket fence
Across from thousands of dead bushes
& marching soldiers
I've tried to paint the time you fell
In front of them
& they trampled you
Without a second thought
I run through a trailer court
Endlessly in the dark
With two rows of florescent lights
On either side
There is not an end to this
Until my limbs are severed
By a man with missing features
& I am left to watch myself in third person
They say that if the plane crashes
I will be crowned the pilot
So I put the oxygen mask on
& hope for the best
I swim to shore in a life vest
& countless people

Fall from captivity in cages
Through trap doors
In the floor
Into Unknown territory
Perhaps freedom
Perhaps worse

I always dream that you're asleep
& then I wake up

CONVERSATION V

"You finally get your chance
To dance on the moon

& your ship breaks down

No way home"

THE MANIA MANIFESTO

Mania
Tells us a thousand lies
Gives us a thousand ideas
Grants us nine distinct lives

To exit such fantastic Filth,
We must sit with the Divine
& barter or bartend
Our way back to Earth

THE TWO: A ~~Poetry~~ Study

By Joseph Colyer

TIME IN THE WORLD

I have all the time in the world
Endless
Diamonds
Ribbons
Pearls

No supply of
Men

But plenty of
Girls

TWENTY-FIRST CENTURY APHRODITE

A twenty-first century
Aphordite
Follow the flowers
You'll always find me

In scorching heat
Or tundras cold,
I'll always show my soul

Though I've lost Forever,
I'll find Another soon

I'll will my petals to wither
So that another's may bloom

Always,

For you.

MARRIED VI

Where I am used to having twice the heart,
I find myself left with one third
The place of my youth
Less a home,
Much more a safe house
Phantoms sleep with me
Where I am used to seeing face
At night, I wonder back
To those familiar, lonely places
& I miss this city
Where I used to be the King
& I can only dream
What would my life be

If I had chosen
To wear that ring?

ARTISTIC HIBERNATION

An artist
Often goes into a type of
Hibernation
Like a dormant volcano;
Pompeii lay in ruin below us
Although not versed in the trade
Of archeology,
It is our job to uncover
Such colossal,
Questionable
Fossils, until our nails bleed:
Our shovels are broken in
Half underground:
The remains of lovers
Left buried in ash,
Set in stone,
& cities bathed in soot,
Long gone,
Before the heat between our Earth's
Plates break again
So that Creation
Accented with destruction and disaster
Can gleefully resume

THE TWO: A ~~Poetry~~ Study

By Joseph Colyer

THE SMALL BOY

The small boy
Fashions a duffel bag
Of large toys

His pants sag
With coins he takes
Across the street

When he enjoys
The company of another Fake
Passion through a gloryhole

I, PRAY

I've forgotten so many faces that
I, Pray that one day

I can only forget yours

THE VERTICAL MIRROR XX

I cannot return to that realm
Without miserable flocks
Blocking my path
Telling me
        "No
        Don't Go"

But venture forth, I will

An omen, I'm sure
Perhaps more
& the blackbirds die
As you murdered all the crows

FIRE ESCAPE

The fire escape
Was truly an escape
It was amazing to climb those stairs

Following me,
She did dare

& at the top,

I
Saw
Her
See
It
Too

POSSIBLE

How is it possible to cherish the embrace;
Of that, which was ***never warm?***

Why is it that we crave such a distant place;
Of which, to us, was ***never foreign?***

MY RELATIONSHIP WITH PHOTOGRAPHY

The boy is fearless,
With his camera and I,
Strapped around his neck

He steals me away to an
Ancient agelessness
That I neglect to forget –

I've never had an eye for photography,
But seeing my realm through his lens,
Forces me to see the world,
Exactly as it is.

RULES

I am waking to see phantoms
That have since replaced the faces
Of the hearts I've held for ransom
& the homes I've found
In the most unfamiliar places

The rules to this game are this:
They're advertised as painless
If you can love someone at random,
You're closer than you know to being

Famous

~~POETRY I~~

We walk with our heads tilted down,
Filled with woe-is-me's
Carrying hearts held heavy
With visceral feelings;
Half our time sleeping:
Veins pulsing full of unfulfilled dreams
Spending our whole lives decaying
In bodies such as these –

So why does no one give a damn
About ~~poetry?~~

GOOD

I've never been one who's Good at keeping secrets

Hell, all of mine are published

THE VERTICAL MIRROR XXII

We know two emotions:
Shame and Terror
Find me here, if you dare

THE TWO: A ~~Poetry~~ Study

By Joseph Colyer

THE FURNACE

I am in love with the machine
In the basement
Every night
She sings me to sleep

Thank you, sweetie

SEX

Sex is a bored game
Usually, it's Sorry

By Joseph Colyer

HEARTBEATS OUT OF UNISON

We never needed to match a face
To a body
A body to a name
A name to an appendage
That shall remain nameless
Eyes in total: four
But two never met
Two
Save for the last time:

Heartbeats out of unison

THE DEFINITION II

I have come to find that Love is fluid.

COUNTLESS SHEEP

All I really want

Is a decent night's sleep

No headaches

No heartbreaks

No counting countless sheep

HOLLOW

Through the cascade of grey,
& my prescription ketamine,
I see – magic:
Passion that poisions, prophetically

> "No one's ever done that to me."
> Trapped in my crystal ball: froze

To you, I am poetry
To me, ***you are*** prose

So, in those two umber irises
I saw foreign,
A far-off field of fiberglass:
A certainty: uncertain
Sorrow and memories
That I've already known
Yet, ***so*** new to me –
Endlessly ***Hollow***
As "infidelity"

AFTERWARDS

I can barely keep my eyes open,

Can hardly keep my mouth shut

TIME WE DON'T HAVE

Questionably worthless;
Futile shit:
Existing with the sole purpose
To simply exist –

Taking up an extra
Six feet of space –
Using up precious air –
A waste of a pretty face,
& time we don't have to spare

SLOWLY

Slowly
Slowly
Slowly
We transfer our pain to
~~Poetry~~

DARLING, DEAR

There's a paradigm shift, these days
I can't describe it any other way
A small voice, although whispered,
Never fails to say:

> "Darling,
> Dear,
> You'll be okay"

MARRIED VII

A colossal diamond revolves around

A ring of rock around space junk

Pulling tidal waves of alcohol

To swim around our junk

~~POETRY II~~

Poetry is never a cry for help
It is so much more than that
It simply calls attention to itself

~~Everyone is sad~~

ON VULNERABILITY

Perpetual vulnerability
Is allowing all irritability
To be visible to irritation

Constant ***vulnerability***
Is no exercise in futility
Living a life, visibly
Is not always pretty

Let alone,
Beautiful

PROVERB

Eyes which scrutinize
Will seldom see

THE VERTICAL MIRROR XXIII

Just when you think you outrun the fear
& a post-someone's soul appears
If you do so dare to endear
I hope you peer into The Vertical Mirror
& see me there

Such sadness
Absent of any tears

"TAKEN"

"Taken"
He says

As the light from his phone
Illuminates

The inside of his pants
Again

PLOT-TWIST

Someone knew Someone new

ALCOHOLISM

I've seen secrets I can't keep
My soul sees from the ceiling;

I can no longer go to sleep
Unless the room is spinning

SELF-AWARE DELUSIONAL

Although my delusions would have written
Different words
My despair is much too self-aware
To feign that I am likely not the first
To pen such similar phrases,
A self-proclaimed
        "Gifted"
        "Cursed"
Or do I come from a species who've settled
For millennium – ages
A seed seething
Into the dirt of the agricultural age
The city's heartbeat pumps
Millennial blood

Strangle me, strange

BREAK MY NECK

He says he's spent months fantasiing
About breaking my neck

In recent days, I'm wondering
How much lips would feel
Against his back

What is it about sex,
That seems better
If you know your heart – to regret?

So, turn the lights down
Restrained, with no sound
So I can hear you

Break my neck.

CONVERSATION VI

"Wisdom can not be bought"

"I pay a pretty price for it"

GENERATION WHY

My generation is a liaison
With a sick fixation
On the future of technology
& the past previous
When the greenery was replaced
For the greenery lining the condensation
Of our ancestors' refrigerators
Unconscious sleeping
Below the floorboards
While we line our pockets
With the blood of the bottles
That line our cabinets and countertops
The next iteration won't read this
But they will try our clothing on –
Doing our dirty laundry
Without checking our pockets
To see what once lined their insides
Is mine
The only generation
To ever ask the forbidden

"Why?"

THE ORIGIN STORY

In the Garden of Eden
My muse was born

I am the second Adam;
I removed my entire rib cage
& blew a kiss into the dirt;

All this fruit, and no fruition,
My Lips are now damnation
& My Touch: forbidden

You ungrateful creation!

My boundless beauty,
& you're unbearably bored?

Still, you drank the poison;
Now you can't untaste the Truth
A sublime mankind is a lie
All thanks to you

I DEMAND MY DUALITY

I enact a series of trials –
To test his validity

An inevitable denial –
Of his inaccessibility

How horrible can I be –
Before he decides to leave?

So I push my polarity –
I demand my duality

THE VERTICAL MIRROR XXIV

Oh!
What a beauty!

Such a gorgeous specimen
Of the human race!
Such masculine confidence;
Such feminine grace!
Such drama; such fury!
A pharmaceutical monument
Someone you can not forget
So humble; such courage!

Would you look at this face?

IT MUST BE HARD

To be soft all the time

THE TWO: A ~~Poetry~~ Study

By Joseph Colyer

ONE, TWO, FOUR

We are disco balls
Endless refractions
Of ourselves
Through The Vertical Mirrors
That adorn our bedroom walls
Lifeless archangels
With four horrible faces
Present to The Waking World:
One
& condemning those
With the nerve to show
Even
Two
Of the immaculate stained glass tiles
Which we paint upon ourselves
In the false privacy of our own homes
Behind screens covered in static
As we stare at our respective
Respected ceilings
Until it is too unnerving
To look at another
& not see the
Tiny

Shiny
Decahedron dice
Hanging from their rear
View

By Joseph Colyer

COLLABORATION

You are cut from a fabric
That I could never wear out

We kiss in this fountain
But I know we'll dry out

But who is to say I won't soon
Find you in the clouds

When, every day
I see you in the sky

THE GRASS IS GREENER

The clouds are in constant cadence
Against supersaturated blue hues
The grass is greener
Because that's how it looks to you

Yet, is it truly greener on the Other Side

Or, would it look much differently
If we were to gaze upon it
Through a higher species eyes?

THE TWO: A ~~Poetry~~ Study

By Joseph Colyer

SHOULD WE?

Should we seek to excavate
The historic past of Yesterday
Perhaps our cause should be
To preserve the face of the fate
Of Tomorrow's golden providence:

Cities sleek
Proverbs honest
The answers to all our unanswered,
Forgotten promises

QUARTER PAST THREE

Songbirds sing
It's a quarter past three
Their vocal chords are

Swollen with
Pollen

I, HOPE

I hope
It breaks
Your heart
When you
Find out
You weren't

Always

The boy
I was
Writing about

I, LIED

For your Love
I’ve written Two

THE TWO: A ~~Poetry~~ Study

By Joseph Colyer

SUBCULTURE

I was only sixteen
When I climbed the staircase
To that place

I walked in to find
Everyone naked
Dressed in lace
Toking on a beautiful piece
Laced
With amphetamines

Souls
Lost
Behind messy makeup

WHITE

I've spilled all my gasoline;
I can't spend the night

I'm dressed in white;
You can't keep me clean

TWO GIFTS

Depression is a weapon
Mania is not misery

They are set of new eyes, with which to see;

Gifts, they could be
If they are used properly

PLANNED

Many smooches await you
Oh, boundless businessman
I have for you, flowers and flowering emotions
That, even you, could not have planned

YOU THINK YOU KNOW A GUY

We only meet a few in our lifetime
On that other side across the line
That divides what we can show
With what we don't wish to know

When we look across the picket fence
Decorated with decadent barbed wire
& grant them even a false sense of respect
We trade places with all we once thought
To be desire

All illusions of their perfections are erased
We now see their soul,
Not their faces

ON WRITING

Writing documents validity;
Estranged from the actual;
In our ocean of emotions,
Feelings can then be proven: factual

There is no nobility in humility;
All things are imaginable
Should we flirt with the notion,
That what is not visible
Is retrievable

THE TWO: A ~~Poetry~~ Study

By Joseph Colyer

USUALLY

He seems to want to know me
But ***what is there to know?***

They're usually simplified into
Bite-size stories
After they've reviewed ***the show***

AS LUCK WOULD HAVE IT

I find I stumble upon black cats
I've run over many crows
I always spill the salt
Ladders turn up – often unexpected
So I've hung a horseshoe over my heart

But, still,
It never fails to melt

THE TWO: A ~~Poetry~~ Study

By Joseph Colyer

GODDESS, FLY

We talk a lot
About being free from each other
Oh, how Venus has wronged us

But Aphrodite has never lied to me;
She has always brought me such souls of Solace
& when she sees fit, drags them
Back to the Nether,
Grants me, yet another, life
So that
I am born
With new eyes;
New wings

& she whispers to me:
"Goddess, Fly"

RECEIPT

Yes, my heart comes with a gift receipt
If you decide you'd like to return

Yes, you may keep my mystique
If I can borrow your charm

QUIVERS

My body quivers
When I possess a Love
Which ***I*** was only meant to borrow

My body is a quiver
Meant to ***carry***
Messenger doves;

Impaled by one too many
Of ***Cupid's arrows***

ON MUSES

A muse mustn't know of their musings.

They always expect a sonnet
Documenting all their beauty
They want to be the king of a painting –
Your play-write

You can not expect to know your beloved subject
Better than the medium will portray.

SOULS

& now we're two different souls
With two different souls

Solely too   Different

TRULY, HUMAN

Room so undecorated and malicious
Eyes so blank and shiny
I could see myself in them
Both
Clothes so decorated and extravagant
That, when removed, proved

Truly, Human

THE TWO: A ~~Poetry~~ Study

By Joseph Colyer

STASIS

We will spend today
Pricking our fingers on the broken glass
Of yesterdays

Most of ***our future***
Glimpsing into the past
& ***wishing that we*** never ***had***

ANTARCTICA

Those eyes
Are the ice
Of Antarctica:
Cold –
Unexplored –
Unprotected –
From man

TELEPATHIC

The wind spoke through the grass

"Not yet"

The birds chimed through the wind

"Be patient"

God lives in human regret:

Telepathic

QUIET

Your kiss
Is a ball gag:

Manufactured
To keep us

Quiet

THE ONLY BOX

He was the only box
Of memories
That wasn't warmed
By fiberglass insulation

He was the only box
I could open
Without doing myself
Any harm

ON PLAGIARISM

Copy,

Paste,

Cut this

The human heart's a plagiarist

PROVERB III

Thresholds built
On pedestals, tall
Will never
Fail to fall

IDEOLOGY

An atheist claims no gods
Then worships Rationalism

HOLY MATRIMONY

They say that cattle
Run into the electric fence
Several times, before they learn

If gasoline was sentient
Would it be aware
That its sole purpose was to be burnt?

They romanticize that black widows
Mate with the same partner for life
Disregarding the parallels of possession
That we humans call affectionately:

Holy matrimony

They say there is a type of bird
That flies with its lover into the sky
Before returning, plummeting, beak-first to Earth

We haven't evolved quite as much
From the captive creatures we enslave
We simply change the names

From stupidity to success
From abuse to beauty
From ritual to ceremony

THE TWO: A ~~Poetry~~ Study

By Joseph Colyer

I, WANDER

When ***I am*** peering into the mirror,
To see if you admire me too,

I, Wander, I wonder,

Is it ***too good to be true,***
Or am I but a foolproof fool?

CHECKOUT LINE

He checks me out

Buying flowers

For his boyfriend

STAR-CROSSED

Our stars were not crossed –

We should not have crossed The Stars.

You can only play god for so long –

Before He reminds you who you are.

CODEWORD

The code to the safe
Is one-four-three

As long as you're with me,
I promise you're safe

The code to the phone
Is one-four-three

We have a bloody code
For everything

A code for amphetamines
A code for the phrase after
You put your hands on me

We have a bloody code
For everything

~~POETRY III~~

~~Poetry~~
Is built to be

Pretentious

VANITY

I believe history
We one day find me

Perhaps a delusional vanity;
But perhaps, a self-fulfilling prophecy

DREAM SEQUENCE CONGLOMERATE

When I was just a kid,
I lost my glasses on the playground
I haven't seen the world clearly ever since
I climb the fence
Into a dark trailer park
Again
With just one light
Visions of a young girl
I could only see in the nighttime
In flashbacks,
He tells me
He sees shadows on the roadside
Of a daughter he's never met
Who keeps him awake at his bedside
A ticking clock we both
Find mildly disturbing
& prevents us from falling asleep
Driving,
She tells me that the water
Is blue
But I can not see it, as she

He waters his flowers with liquor
To drink at a later date
Because rose-stained vodka
Is his only hope
At romantic arousal
Piloting a plane
Into the depths of the ocean
Hollow
Hollow,
Seems to be a theme
& that truth that I won't swallow

ON REINVENTING TRAUMA

If we are not careful,
We reinvent memories –
Distorting time in real-time –
Cogs in our machinery
Crank themselves alive
Before we can bid them goodbye,
We remove the spine,
Replacing it with the severed vertebrae
Of countless yesterdays –
Modified to soil today

With traumas we can't reimagine properly

INFANCY

We are told in our infancy
Until our adulthood
That we are special –
Without a question –
That we are capable of anything
Before delusions of grandeur
Can speak
Such similar sweet ***nothings*** to us

VENGEANCE

We all want revenge
But none has been so sweet

As another man on his knees –

Reciting your poetry

I AM NOT

I am not your artist
I will not make you beautiful

I am not your guardian angel
I will not keep you safe

JUDGMENT DAY

What good is better judgment –
When we are at our happiest

On Judgment Day

ANALOG CLOCK

The clock on my way
Can't decide what second it is –

Not like it used to –

I won't buy
Batteries to fix it

THE TWO: A ~~Poetry~~ Study

By Joseph Colyer

NOIR

It was a noir film:

Too silent to be heard

A poem, set into prose:

Not enough words

THE VERTICAL MIRROR XXV

Whatever worlds lived before,
They don't exist for us anymore

I will build no immortal portals –
No more woodless doors

But you know where to find me,
Where the gardens once were

I've left a breadcrumb trail of roses
If your mind doesn't mind the thorns

If you're sharp enough
To follow them –

Of all the gateways closed,
There remains,

Just one

THE TWO: A ~~Poetry~~ Study

By Joseph Colyer

'NEATH THE COVER OF NIGHT

The tapping ***always*** comes
From my front door
Once I've ***shut***
Off ***the*** lights
& already crawled under –
'Neath the cover of night

Like faceless solicitors
Asking me if I know Christ,
It lifts a ***shadow*** to my window:
That famous dull knife
& commits the sin
That many have:
Spilling ***out*** to me, its insides

Leaving no more secrets
Left to hide

'Neath the cover of night

NEW YORK CITY

Aliens walk the streets
Of New York City
All their facial features
Show too much symmetry

Hardened loins –
Harder muscles

As if they've studied us for years –
Observing our perceived notion of ideals;
Their research funneled
Into false idols –

Carvings –
Cravings

Of all-too iridescent statues of marble

THE TWO: A ~~Poetry~~ Study

By Joseph Colyer

THE PATHOGEN

Sleep is the pathogen
That ***our souls*** contract

With every wish to die

Dreams ***are*** the oxygen
That keep our lungs alive

Carrying us on clouds,
Again and again

To the next sunrise
Taken for granted

GOOD GIRLS

Boys are for toys

& nihilism's all for show

Good girls like God,

Vanity & clothes

Hearts – as much a mystery

As solving yellowed snow

I SPOKE TO GOD

I spoke to God
To tell him life is not fair
They, as always, told me to look around
& I asked
"Where?"
They said
"Do you see where the trees
Meet the air?"
Do you see yourself crossing busy streets
Without a fear?
You see,
It's all statistically impossible,
My dear,
Yet here we are,
Joseph,
Life is not fair"

EVOLUTION

Under the facade of sophistication,
& pseudo-intellectual communications,
We are balding gorillas
With power tools
& an alphabet

HE, ONLY

He,
Only writes poems in the rain

He,
Only smiles on the train

He,
Only hears you
When he can't quite make out

What it is you're saying

FILLED THE ROOM

I've filled the room with flowers
Of Forever
So you must
Make me out to be kind –

If you thought I didn't know roses
To Wither,
Just you watch me
Watch them die

POPULAR OPINION

If you adopt a popular opinion,
Was it ever your opinion?

–isms
Are just religions
That call a cause their God

ARE WE HEALING?

Are we healing,
Or just slowly forgetting?

THE TWO: A ~~Poetry~~ Study

By Joseph Colyer

LOST AMONGST HIS CARPET FIBERS

His eyes carve hallways
Into the Dark
Carvings etch a story on his back
My diamond earrings:
Lost amongst his carpet fibers

& every fiber of my being he calls
~~Poetry~~

As he pours another drink
Into an insulated cup of aluminum –
Isolated

He tells me tales
As sweet
As the grain alcohol
He would happily trade
A communion plate
Of stale bread for –
By mourning

But a passing, blind glimpse
Out of the tattered and bruised blinds

Would prove
That was already the hour

THE VERTICAL MIRROR XXVI

He pulls the curtain

Back   between

The granite staircase
& a world much less regal
Where candles Light the way
& televisions only play channels
Infected with dynamic static

ALL MY LOVE

All my love is public
You'll find it in your luggage

Very
        Very
                Soon

My darling, poor thing
Its pages shall be a mirror reflecting the

Truth

Yet you will ache to craft them –

Every
        Sonnet

Every
        Passage

Into mere flattery ***for you***

THE TWO: A ~~Poetry~~ Study

By Joseph Colyer

APPARITION

I leave

Like an apparition
Leaves the body
Of a newly deceased corpse

Like the unfortunate afternoon
When the moon exit
The orbit of the Earth

Like the safe haven
Of a mother's womb
Forgotten after birth

Like the stars
Leave the sky
When the sun returns

TERRIFIED

Nothing half-good has ever happened
Paralyzed by perfection

TRANSACTION

We're tithed to one another
By mortgages and taxes

We've learned to treat Love
As a business transaction

WARM

Angels kept me warm
When the cold came through the walls

But,
When your body,
The angels were you,
All along –

I should have kept you warm
        I should have kept you warm
                I should have kept you warm
I should have kept you warm
        I should have kept you warm
                I should have kept you warm
I should have kept you warm
        I should have kept you warm
                I should have kept you warm

I PRAY MY SIGNATURE IS ALWAYS WORTH NOTHING

The legacy of
The Forlorn ***Artist***
Should never have to be
A bonafide tragedy

If only
The contents
Of our visions – Most sincere
Were to ***be revered***
Before the public
Is told that they must be

I, A SUNKEN SHIP

You were the statue of civil liberty
Waste-deep in the ocean
The welcome committee
To the city with open arms –
A bottle of liquor
& a Bible

I, a sunken ship
Carrying precious cargo
& the virus of freedom
That soon went viral

As I climbed the staircase
Into your head
Speaking to a heart
Forever under construction
Covered by
          "No Trespassing"
Signs
& the broken metal
Of not-so-carefully
Closed doors

THE TWO: A ~~Poetry~~ Study

By Joseph Colyer

THE HORRORS

A lover once told me
That The Horrors
Will lead a man to do unspeakable,
Impossible
Things

I've spent forever dissecting what that means
In my quest, I've been dramatic,
But, judging by what I've seen,
We are all mortified of absolutely everything –

How you'd sound in the shower,
If you dared to sing

Your dead stepfather,
Who still visits you when you sleep

That disease you always consider,
As it runs in your genes

What happens next,
If you give her the ring

Where you'd end up,
If you couldn't renew the lease

What he might be packing,
Inside of his jeans

How the world will react,
To our new Celebrity King

If you're one to follow,
Or one to lead

At the end of the day,
Your dreams are only dreams

& worst of all,
Although, painfully, it may sting:

How are we,
As a culture
To survive
Times like these?

NOT GOOD

I know today
Will not be good

The carpet fibers
Have begun to play
Leap frog

The furnace
Speaks to me
In tongues

The letters on my phone
Replace themselves
With scores of music
I've yet to have heard before

I am Home alone –
This house comes alive
To keep me company

CONVERSATION VII

"Don't you find it depressing;
Not having a shred of faith
In the Divine?"

"Quite the opposite.
We are alive,
Procreate,
Die,
Then, our atoms are recycled
Into the void infinity of Space.

There's so much beauty in that, babe;
That's the hope that gets me through
The Day."

THE TWO: A ~~Poetry~~ Study

By Joseph Colyer

DARLING

Darling, your eyes
Have ever met mine
I've likely turned you into
A slant rhyme

& not a particularly good one

THE THREE

I take cheap blows at him,
As he buys blow from him,
Before blowing me

A vicious cycle
The kind of morbid love triangle
You'd find in a movie,

Or a porno,
If you're lucky

THE RELATIONSHIP STUDY MANIFESTO

We all crave romance
Or, at the very least,
Intimacy –

For, when the moment ***is*** all but passed,
Of ***our furthest measure***, we can reach
Into humanity's most human variety
Of insanity

That, when pieced together,
Enters peace.

ANOTHER WOULDN'T CARE

The heart is a masochist
The mind is cruel
I brew your coffee;
You cook me food

We won't shower together
But aren't afraid to use
The other's shampoo
Uncertainly amused
& certainly mused

Terrified,
Half-playing half a House
Feigning that it's just us Two

As dead to us
As the grass of harsh winters
Passed without you
& the snow of letting go

Of the man you never knew
& the most beautiful mind
That another wouldn't care to

CLASSIC ADDICT

He chose his drug
Over you

They always do

WISHED YOU WELL

I wished you well

& it would seem

That my wish came true

That's all I ever really wanted for you

ALMOST NATURAL

I evaporate from existence
I am the condensation you lap
From the rim of your glass

Then I cover you in the shower,
An almost natural cycle

GANGRENE

Sometimes you feel like gangrene
There's not a doubt in my mind
That I would amputate
All my appendages

If it meant I could set you free,
I would leave
In a sawed-off hearse

Adorned with powdered pixies
& dead roses
That never quite
Made ***love*** concise

Enough for me

PSEUDO-INTELLECTUAL

If pleasure is pain –

If Love is Hollow –

If beauty is a face –

If our time is borrowed –

Is our joy today
Only our sorrow tomorrow?

AFTER

He was the love of my afterlife

A heaven –
A hell

On Earth

UNTITLED V

I love you so bad

That nothing good can come of it

LOLITAS

We are a warehouse full
Of broken dolls –

Lolitas left to rot in the corner
Of the frigid
Air-conditioned room –

Precious, painted porcelain faces

Possessed by an evil greater
Than men
Dressed in the garments of yesterday's horrors

ALL IS FAIR

If you love a whore.

CONVERSATION VIII

"We are Sid and Nancy –

Trying to escape the ending"

FAST

It always happens so fast,
Failing to make sense – unless

Just a convenient guise

For time to pass –

Into the past

CONVERSATION IX

"I'm hurting you
Like someone
Trying their best
To make you happy"

MAUSOLEUM

You don't throw it out
Just because you had sex on it, idiot

That's not a stain,
It's a Mausoleum to Pain

ACT NATURAL

He locks the deadbolt -
Fashions a blue flannel

He removes his designer belt
Before whispering –

"Act natural"

HOLY GHOST

The damned
& the angels

Use my body
As a wishbone

A test, to win
My Holy Ghost

SCALE

A bright idea!
Write this,

Hurry!
          Scurry!
                    Away!

A scale that weighs,
How much trauma
You can stomach
Throughout the day!

CENSORED

The say
The best artists get censored

Lucky for you,
I leave much to be desired

THE DEVIL

The devil
Moans in your ear
Sweet promises

Perfection

While God
Offers
A, much less sexy, intervention

The devil
Is a tempest
Of temptations
In
Rapid
Succession

While the angel
On your shoulder
SHOUTS

"Just fucking learn your lesson!"

I, VOW

My medications
Look likes shards of glass

I vow that they may cut my throat

CRIB

4 A M

My bed is a crib
That I have outgrown

A TACKY ROLLER COASTER METAPHOR

You'll find it the most thrilling roller coaster
You've ever ridden –

Until you can't
Get off.

SEX, LIFE

You may be surprised to find
That writing about your sex life
Does wonders for it

BOTH

By your bedside you will see a note

"See you in another life"
Or
"All my love"

They are both

The same

THEN, IT WASN'T

If you feel lighter,
When you loosen your grip,
Then it wasn't meant to
                                        Be

So sad you have to end it
To know if you are
                                        Free

CONVERSATION X

“Relationships are like smoking

Chemicals,
Dependency,
Habit,

Until one is not enough”

THE DUALITY MANIFESTO

Of what we see,
Should we change anything?

A Minimalist nightmare
Is a Dadaist's dream

UNTITLED VII

Well,
I haven't cut my ear off yet

& I can't decide

If that means I still don't love you enough
Or if I haven't lost my mind

ALL I DO

All I do
Is get drunk

& wish it was with you

UNTITLED VIII

It feels

So
Good

To say goodbye

AIR

No use looking for ***love***

It ***is in the air*** about you

UNTITLED IX

It's a full honeymoon phase tonight

THE VERTICAL MIRROR XXVII

If, of the Dark,
You have no fear
Meet me here
On the opposite side
Of The Vertical Mirror

UNTITLED X

& all your ghosts
Were my writers

POETRY BREEDS

Romance
Breeds
Poetry
Romance
Breeds
Poetry
Romance
Breeds
Poetry
Romance
Breeds
Poetry
Romance
Breeds
Poetry
Romance
Breeds
Poetry
Romance
Breeds
Poetry

BIPOLAR DISORDER II

To be bipolar
Is to live two lives
That you don't get to choose –

Constantly mourning
A friend
You never thought you'd lose –

Outgrowing a pair
While trying to fill
Another's shoes

& a noose
Constantly in full view

THIS IS NOT A POEM

Though you claim it not to be,
A pipe is still a pipe

THE MOVIE STAR DELUSION II

We are all in a noir film;
God is watching you pretend to feel

There are cameras at your feet;
Voice recorders in your pillowcase

This isn't real, movie star
The world will forget you

HOLE

They were Courtney and Kurt
I was the shot that slaughtered him
& the legend that followed her

She was my Hole
World

THE ARTIST'S RESPONSIBILITY

It is the Artist's responsibility
To gaze into The Infinite Infinity

Without
Outgrowing their infancy

TOMORROW WON'T

Tomorrow won't remember

What is now, is not forever

Today will ***be better***

~~POETRY IV~~

An English scholar once told me
My prose was vague
& left no room for discovery

Funny

How an expert in writing
Can be so blind to the very breath of

~~Poetry~~

ASHES, DUST

In the morning, I sense you:
The cold, tiled floor of a bathroom

Malice,
Thirst

Vivaldi, played terribly out of tune:

Ashes,
Dust

THE TWO: A ~~Poetry~~ Study

By Joseph Colyer

CONVERSATION XI

"If you love him,
Tell him"

THE VERTICAL MIRROR XXVIII

At times ***I feel***, I don't deserve
To be in the body piloted by this mind
With such a boundless view of ***this world***

THE TWO: A ~~Poetry~~ Study

By Joseph Colyer

I, IMPOSTER

Do I need a permit to be a poet?

TO THE AUTHOR,

In this blank space,
Do not feign authority –

What you write will come to life;

Best to tread carefully.

THE TWO: A ~~Poetry~~ Study

By Joseph Colyer

THEORY

In theory,
If to keep, you were not mine
Would not modify
My heart to beat any different –

But to see it in its entirety,
With my own two eyes?

It absolutely destroyed me –
A disaster deep within my psyche;
An evening feigning eternity
In catatonic catastrophe

SEAGULLS

You see me watching seagulls –
You shake me,
You ask me:

"Darling,
What are you always thinking about?"

I simply say:

"Paris"

& you laugh

Then you take my picture
To capture
The transition

Between

Knowing everything
&, of everything, without

THE TWO: A ~~Poetry~~ Study

By Joseph Colyer

TO MY BELOVED,

My Beloved is gone now
Locked away
In some far-off padded room
Passing up food
Having under her tongue
Checked for cocktails of medication
Electroshock appointments every other weekend
While she's on this happy, little vacation
We insist on exploring her house
To find a bathtub baked with rust
Every surface full of dust,
& a complex system of organized sadness

A lack of empathy; no sense of family.

My Beloved, I understand
The terrified world that you live in
The delusion: everyone is watching
& now that you're gone
They're all talking about fucking
Nothing

But I see you more than I'd like to

Here in The Vertical Mirror,
Everything tastes like shit
There's nothing in your stomach,
But you want to vomit
You want to be on Mars,
Yet here we're stuck on Earth
Though it could easily be mistaken for Hell,
While they preach to us of a Heaven
As if, we haven't met those Horrors too
We see endless phantoms
As we search for a familiar face
Who we can assign a previous life
& recognize a previous time
That we may or may not have even occupied

You were that beauty for me
But you're too far gone
To teach me how to differentiate between
Ghosts and flesh
I fear that you're a premonition:
A future for me;

But though it costs so much sanity

TO MY BELOVED, (CONT.)

To see such dismally, cosmic things
I vow to use these powers

So much differently.

ANYWAY

I feel terrible
Exploiting my exploits

But I'm doing it anyway

AGORAPHOBIA

Every time I leave the house
It feels as though I may never return

UNTITLED XI

It has somehow always been easier
To sleep in a single-sized bed,

With no pressure to fill the opposite side

THE TWO: A ~~Poetry~~ Study

By Joseph Colyer

WHY IS SHE HERE?

She brushes aside her long,
Blond hair
To conceal that we all know
Why she came here

THE VERTICAL MIRROR X

This place has turned to Ether.

~~POETRY V~~

Poetry

Slip
Slip
Slipping
Away;

If you don't

Quickly,

Find the

Write

Words to say

CONVERSATION XII

"The mentally ill worry
About things

Others will never have

To"

UNDERWATER

The moon waned
& waxed
As he poured wax
Across the mane
On the back
Of my neck –

Holding my

Head, underwater

YOU WILL KNOW

You will know where I've been

I leave behind
Coffee rings,
Acrylic stains,
& ashes

THE TWO: A ~~Poetry~~ Study

By Joseph Colyer

THE DAYLIGHT LIFE

"Are you wearing dress pants?!"

He exclaims,
Confused,
Head cocked
To the side –

Either to taunt me with the bruises
He had earned
From the boy
Whose name he could not recall
The night prior

Or out of a genuine
Shock
That, when rolling,
The camera, did stop

How could one return
To The Daylight Life –

Without a second thought?

TO THE NEW GUY,

Run.

While you still can

<u>Feel</u>
<u>Your</u>
<u>Feet</u>

THE TWO: A ~~Poetry~~ Study

By Joseph Colyer

IF

If,
By the score of my songs,
The words were dawned

To you,
They don't belong

Go, write
Your own
Wrongs.

I MISS YOU OFTEN

– Quiet introspection.

UNTITLED XII

You say that word

"Forever"

But no man could ever
Own me for that long
You say that love
Last even after they put
That casket for two
Into the ground

But, darling,
Love happens right now

Not the future
Nor the past
The beauty that is Love

Is that it isn't built to last

"Forever"

MY MIND IS AN AIRPORT

My mind is an airport:

Too many people

Too many officials

Too much baggage being
claimed

Too many machines with wings

Too many assholes

Too many cavity searches

THE TWO: A ~~Poetry~~ Study

By Joseph Colyer

THE END

Finite,
Ended,
Abruptly over:

The petals off a wilted rose;
The last muddy mess of snow
That faint twinkle – always in his eyes,
Before he stretches out his arm

Goodnight.

& so I gaze one last time,
Into The Vertical Mirror
To find the world is not melting.
This Realm is not of Fauvism,
But what his camera has always seen:

Not beautiful Delusion – but blissful Sanity
Not horrible Utopia – but wonderful Reality

Finite,
Ended,
Abruptly over

Closure –
Without –
Closure

JOSEPH COLYER

GRAPHIC DESIGNER

JosephColyerDesign.com

In Memory Of

Joseph Nathan Colyer

March 19, 1996 - September 14, 2021

Printed in the United States of America

Special Edition, 2022

ISBN: 978-1-955498-01-2

Press Here
410 S Michigan Ave
Suite 420
Chicago, IL 60605

In commemoration of Joseph's writing, the hand-drawn elements in this edition illustrate the edits they intended to make to their book. Uncertain of the exact changes that would have been made, Joseph's notes are included to remain true to their vision.